Alien Robot Banker

Marketing with a Twist:
How Humor Can
Transform Your Business

Cordell Giesen

Contents

Introduction
Why
This
Guy?

Introduction: Why this guy?

I have spent over two decades navigating the tumultuous waters of the marketing world. In that time, I've seen a lot – from cringe-worthy marketing campaigns to stroke-of-genius ads that set the town abuzz.

As the years rolled by, I began to notice a troubling trend. Businesses, both big and small, were falling prey to the siren song of average and too often bad creative in their marketing campaigns. It was like watching a parade of clunky slogans and uninspired graphics march through the streets, leaving behind a trail of disappointed customers and dwindling sales. But through the smoke there was a small band of buccaneers marching to their own tune: these brave swashbucklers are having more fun than a pirate singing sea shanties! I wanted to join in.

Determined to help others change the narrative around their marketing results, I embarked on a quest to save those willing to grow from the clutches of marketing mediocrity. Armed with my trusty laptop and a brilliant eye for business benefits, I set out to revolutionize the way businesses approach marketing.

An Unexpected Solution

My mission is simple yet profound: to acknowledge the power of humor in marketing and the urgent need to make it more accessible. No more cookie-cutter ads or recycled slogans – I'm here to inject a dose of guidance and authenticity through humor into *every campaign.*

My greatest reward is seeing the soothing relief wash over their faces, and the spark of fun reignited in the eyes of business owners, fellow marketers, and their clients. Throughout my career, as I started to rack up wins with successful marketing campaigns using humor, I realized something. With each client's success story, I knew that I was one step closer to my ultimate goal: a world where marketing wasn't just good – it was unforgettable, fun and profitable.

I'm geared up with a passion and commitment to help you achieve excellence. Within this book, I will share everything I've learned. I will, additionally, continue on my quest to learn and grow with you so we all benefit from this shared quest. Harness the power of humor for your business and wield it wisely my friends, while at the same time reaping the fun and playful rewards.

What is humor's role in marketing?

Picture this: you're chilling in sunny Los Angeles, dodging palm trees while dreaming of the big time, when suddenly, bam! You're hit with an ad so boring it's like watching paint dry. And just like that it's gone from your mind faster than a hotdog at a baseball game. Here's the problem - that's how most ads are. Most ads are average at best.

That's when you start creating a new plan. That's when you start creating a new *marketing* plan. Your marketing can do more than just sell stuff; marketing should be about making your business shine brighter than a disco ball at a rave. If you want to stand out in a sea of competitors, you need to do more than just give information. Your brand can have a personality that people like. Your brand needs to be memorable. That's the problem with most ads: there is nothing to remember.

I get it. If it was easy, everyone would be doing it. But hold onto your VIP fun passes, because here's the kicker: there are solutions that most marketers either don't understand or think are too hard to apply. I'm talking about humor in business; and more importantly, the formulas and steps that you can immediately start using to help your business.

Alright, let's get this party started!

Storytelling is very powerful. It has created some of the biggest industries on the planet, like movies, publishing, and most of the strongest, most valuable companies in the world. Wait, I thought we were talking about humor? We are. But we're all running at warp speed, and ain't nobody got time for a marathon story with a lot of build up, character development, and everything else that makes a great story. That's where humor swoops in to save the day delivering the message faster than you can say, "beginning, middle, end!". Humor is the ultimate storyteller, squeezing a whole saga into a simple setup and punchline. No long-winded tales here - just quick, snappy messages that stick in your brain like a catchy tune on repeat.

Thanks for joining me. I promise you won't be disappointed.

✔ Bonus Guide:
Humor in Marketing Tool Kit.

Get examples and insights on how to use the concepts in the book to create better marketing campaigns by using the formulas and strategies of Humor in Marketing.

What's Included?
1. The Humor in Marketing Starter Kit
2. The Humor in Marketing Cheat Sheet
3. The Humor in Marketing Scorecard

AlienRobotBanker.com/toolkit

01

Humor
And
Marketing

Two Powerful
Forces Unite

CHAPTER ONE

Humor and Marketing - Two Powerful Forces Unite

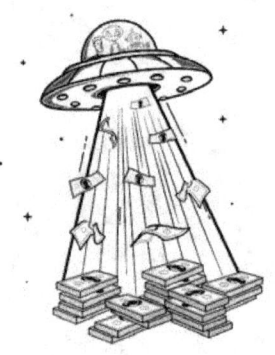

Let's throw some punches!

Humor is the secret sauce that grabs your attention and makes companies grow. Humor is talked about and shared. Humor can amplify the messages of your business. So, why are you not using humor effectively? You're probably not using humor because you don't know how. Here's the good news: Humor is about **formulas** and **strategies** that have been polished and proven effective for centuries. Anyone can learn to use humor for their business. With social media and overall online consumption of, well, everything, it's easier than ever to get your name out there. But the problem is there's more competition too.

You need an edge. That's why you need to learn the ins and outs of humor and how to apply it to your business.

Why humor? It all starts when you're just a little baby. The good ol' days of early childhood, where laughter was the currency of love, friendship and fun. Humor is the glue that holds us all together! From those first giggles with our parents to laughing out loud with our friends and family, humor has always been a trusty sidekick. With the challenges of life, humor is something that most people not only appreciate, but crave more of. In short, humor works as a tool for your business to get more customers.

Here's the idea: You wouldn't cook great food without some spices! So let's find some marketing spice to spice up how you communicate to your customers. Let's make your business pop by working with emotions.

But aren't there risks? Not if you know what you're doing. This book is your guide to avoiding risk and keeping your customers happy and coming back for more. Quit paying for impressions. It's time to start creating impressions.

The emotions of laughter, happiness and fun, together known as humor, is like a magical magnet that grabs your customer's attention and refuses to let go. It's the super hero of your marketing, turning mundane ads into moments you'll never forget while laughing all the way to the bank.

Study after study shows us that adding a touch of emotion and humor to ads can make them more engaging, memorable, and give people a better feeling about the brand.

It's all about finding the right balance between making someone laugh and making them feel connected to what's being advertised. There is a right and a wrong way to do this. Formulas and proven techniques, detailed in this book, will guide you and show you how crucial it is to your success to correctly mix humor and emotions in ads.

So, grab your measuring stick and get ready for some marketing magic, because we're about to dissect the hilarious success stories of brands like Geico, Old Spice, and Dollar Shave Club, as well as several smaller brands to show it's not the budget, but the strategy that is the key ingredient. Yep, we're diving deep into the belly of the humor beast to uncover the secret sauce behind their side-splitting campaigns. We're even going to measure whether it's all worth it or not. But first, let's start with a few basics.

Start with the right tools.

Humor is a marketing tool that shows that your brand values the customers they serve and are willing to stop wasting their customers' time. Successful and lucrative brands entertain their customers in exchange for attention. Then, they get to do business with them.

Most marketers think the goal of marketing is to promote and sell products or services by understanding and influencing consumer behavior. However, influencing is only part of the challenge. It's about making an impression, not measuring impressions. Many marketers never get the chance to be heard.

It's now too easy to skip over most ads. As a good marketer, you need to grab the attention of your audience. In most cases, you have to capture their attention in less than ten seconds. It's not just about being polished with pretty pictures and professional production, it's about grabbing attention and making a connection.

According to marketing experts such as Gary Vaynerchuck and others, **the number one reason marketers fail to make an impression is because businesses don't care enough.** In many communities and regions of the world, you can't even start talking to someone about business unless you humanize yourself first. This is especially true in marketing where customer skepticism, cynicism, and short attention spans dominate the landscape. Most businesses forget to show they care about their customers, or show that they value them. So how can we, as marketers, show that we value our customers and truly care about them? You guessed it. With humor. It shows you spent the time to earn their attention and trust.

Marketing as entertainment

One of the best ways to create a bond with your audience is to give them something first, namely offering value in the form of entertainment, before asking for something in return. With marketing through entertainment, we can use the power of emotions for better ad results. We can leverage emotions to gain attention, engagement, action, and to increase recall.

Emotions enhance memory by creating stronger and more lasting connections in the brain. Ads that evoke feelings are more likely to be remembered, and will produce more positive decisions around your products and services. Yep, we're talking about more sales here. Most purchasing decisions are influenced by emotions over rational analysis. Connecting emotionally can sway consumer decisions in favor of an advertised product or service. This creates a long term brand connection and lends to brand loyalty, which leads to more sales, better reviews, and recommendations.

The sharing of positive opinions about your company is very valuable, and often is the difference between massive success and failure. Ads that evoke strong emotions are also more likely to be shared with friends, family and coworkers, increasing their reach and impact beyond the initial audience. When you have something that makes the person sharing it look better, you're more likely to have it spread. By tapping into emotions, marketers can effectively engage with their audience, enhance their brand's appeal, and drive consumer behavior.

Marketing is not a feature length movie

Now, before we continue, let's get one thing straight: we're not making a feature-length rom-com movie here. In the world of marketing, it's all about cutting to the chase and hitting 'em with the punchline faster than you can say "thank you for what you do for me!" It's effective because of how quickly you can get laughs, connections and results.

Humor and laughter are an aspect of emotion that is uniquely suited for advertising. One interesting piece of research used special methods to watch and understand people's facial expressions while they were experiencing ads. The study concluded that the way ads make us feel, especially when they make us laugh, plays a large part in how effective those ads are.

Audience Agreement

In the Harvard Business Review's article, "The New Rule of Marketing Across Channels", the authors discuss the importance of the "echoverse". The HBR article defines the echoverse as "a complex web of feedback loops and reverberations that are created by consumers, brands, news media, investors, communities, society, and artificial intelligence (AI) agents". The main takeaway from the HBR article is: How can we amplify our marketing messages? Is your audience enjoying your ads, talking about your ads, and sharing them with others? This is important so you get more mileage out of your efforts. It's not just a want anymore, it's how marketing is done today. But first you have to earn their respect. I call this the audience agreement. We'll delve further into how we can do this later. The reason we do this is so we can put your customers to work getting you more customers by way of followers, shares, and positive interactions with your marketing campaigns.

---

[1] https://hbr.org/2024/06/the-new-rules-of-marketing-across-channels

We've already discussed how using humor in your marketing produces ads that evoke strong emotions. Ads that use humor are more likely to be shared, increasing their reach and impact beyond the initial audience. Is it possible to get more bang for your buck than a pony packed piñata at a birthday bash? With humor in your marketing mix, it's not only possible, it's inevitable. When people share your ads it's like hitting the jackpot. And what gets shared more than a cat wearing sunglasses? You guessed it —humor! We'll also break down why and how you can create your own sunglass wearing cat that aligns with your brand, campaign and company goals a little later.

Let's sprinkle some humor into this marketing mix!

People don't just buy the product, they buy the story behind the product. Think of brands like Liquid Death, Nike, and Apple. They use storytelling. But in marketing, there's an even more efficient way to use storytelling. It's still storytelling, just a specific kind of storytelling: It's humor.

Brands can, and should, effectively utilize humor in their advertising campaigns to engage audiences and enhance brand recall.

Here are some notable examples:

1. **Geico** - Geico's advertising strategy heavily relies on humor across various formats, from their famous gecko mascot to scenarios depicting absurdly easy ways "Geico could save you 15% or more on car insurance".

Their commercials often feature unexpected twists and characters, such as cavemen and talking animals, which keep viewers entertained and engaged.

2. **Burger King** - Burger King has employed humor through various stunts and social media campaigns. For example, their mock proposal to McDonald's to create a "McWhopper" for Peace Day combined humor with a message of unity, catching the public's attention.

3. **IKEA** - IKEA's ads often include light-hearted, humorous takes on the everyday challenges people face with assembling furniture and organizing their homes. Their campaigns are known for playful digs at their own complicated assembly instructions.

These examples illustrate how humor is a powerful tool in advertising, making ads more memorable and enjoyable for the audience.

These brands demonstrate the power of storytelling in marketing, but with a twist. The brands are leveraging compelling narratives to engage audiences, build emotional connections, and differentiate themselves in competitive markets.

That's why your business needs to create a fun and playful environment for your customers. As a marketer, adding humor to your arsenal is not just a good idea—it's downright essential. Let's face it: in a world where every ad looks the same, standing out is how you get ahead.

Humor for your business is something to be embraced. We're not taking risks. This is Spongebob level humor. Family humor. Wordsmith and word play humor. Not Bevis and Butthead or Southpark humor. We'll go over how to avoid pitfalls later in this book.

When considering adding humor to your business and marketing, you should really think of it as the super glue of humanity. Humor binds us together; It breaks the ice and makes life just a little bit brighter. That is why humor is so attractive.

When incorporating humor into your marketing, we'll treat it as though we are providing a map to a decision your customers will be more inclined to take. The decision your prospective customers will want to make over and over again is to do business with you. People don't choose between things, they choose between descriptions of things. Your description must evoke emotion. This is why marketing was created. Many businesses don't leverage marketing's true potential.

One of the most powerful emotions for business to harness is humor. Humor in marketing uses structure to surprise and delight the audience. By leading the audience one way, like a magician, the focus is then changed in a way that the audience doesn't see what is coming. The surprise releases tension and creates a long lasting, appreciated and shareable moment. Adding your brand to the gag is how you get your audience to consider choosing you as a solution to their problems.

The best marketing campaigns are like pollen. They stick around and spread. What's your pollen? If you want your ideas to stick around and spread, then using a strategy that has been connecting people to one another for thousands of years is something that you can also use to help your business. This will not only make your job more fun, but it will also make the world a better place.

Trio of Tutors

So, how are we going to be able to confidently add humor to our marketing and business? With some guidance, of course. To help us get everything organized, let's use some worthy experts as our guides. It's time to grab your popcorn and meet our trusty business guides. This trio of humor and marketing specialists will lead you to the promised lands of fun, connections and cashflow.

The Alien, the Robot, and the Banker: A Fable of Humorous Success

Once upon a time in the bustling city of Biztopia, an alien named Zog, a robot named Byte, and a banker named Mr. Coin all lived together. Each of them had a unique talent that could help businesses thrive using the power of humor.

Zog, the alien, came from a distant planet called Laughon, where humor was the essence of life. Zog had an extraordinary ability to teach the basics of humor. One day, Zog gathered a group of eager business owners and said, "Humor is like a universal language that breaks barriers and builds connections. It's as simple as a well-timed joke or a clever pun. Use humor to make your brand relatable and memorable."

The business owners were fascinated, but they wanted to delve deeper. Enter **Byte the robot**, programmed with an encyclopedic knowledge about the intricacies of humor in marketing. Byte rolled in with a whirr and a click, displaying data and charts. "Humor in marketing," Byte explained, "involves understanding humor formulas and techniques, using relevant cultural references, and creating a relationship. It's about knowing when to be witty and when to be subtle. Humor should align with your brand's voice and values."

The business owners nodded, appreciating the detailed guidance. But then they asked, "How do we know if our humor is working?" That's when **Mr. Coin, the banker**, stepped in. With a sharp suit and an even sharper mind, Mr. Coin knew how to measure success. "The key," he said, "is in the metrics. Track engagement rates, monitor social media reactions, and measure changes in brand perception. Look at the bottom line—did sales increase after a humorous campaign? Use data to refine your approach and ensure that humor translates into tangible results."

The trio—Zog, Byte, and Mr. Coin—formed an unbeatable team. With Zog's foundational teachings, Byte's detailed formulas and strategies, and Mr. Coin's analytical insights, businesses in Biztopia flourished. They learned that humor, when used wisely, could transform their marketing and lead them to unparalleled success.

And so in Biztopia, laughter and business growth went hand in hand thanks to the wisdom of an alien, a robot, and a banker. As the businesses celebrated their success, Zog quipped, "Who knew making money could be so funny?"

Byte responded, "Just remember, when in doubt, laugh it out!"

Mr. Coin added with a chuckle, "And always keep a joke in your pocket—right next to your wallet!"

✓ Bonus Guide:
Humor in Marketing Tool Kit.

Get examples and insights on how to use the concepts in the book to create better marketing campaigns by using the formulas and strategies of Humor in Marketing.

What's Included?
1. The Humor in Marketing Starter Kit
2. The Humor in Marketing Cheat Sheet
3. The Humor in Marketing Scorecard

AlienRobotBanker.com/toolkit

Ready, set, don't forget...

_____

_____

_____

_____

_____

_____

_____

_____

_____

_____

_____

_____

_____

_____

_____

_____

_____

_____

_____

_____

_____

_____

02

Alien
Robot
The Banker

Your Guides
To
Marketing With Humor

CHAPTER TWO

Alien, Robot, and The Banker - Your Guides to Marketing With Humor

The **Alien**, the **Robot**, and the **Banker** are the companions who will lead you. With **Zog, the alien, Byte,** the robot, and **Mr. Coin,** the banker, we'll journey through the mystical land of humor formulas and techniques, which through guided practice, will turn you into a humor hero. Soon you'll be getting clients faster than you can say "Peter piper picked a peck of pickled peppers." No more hunting around for the right marketing plan, we've got everything you need right here; laid out like a stack of bills so thick you could use it as a makeshift mattress. Now that sounds comforting! Let's make your brand the life of the party, one laugh at a time.

When your audience is laughing, your business is winning. And who doesn't want to be on the winning team?

Let's face it, customers and audiences are skeptical. And with good reason. They've been talked to in so many different ways it's down right confusing. Humor has the power to use playful language to disarm and connect.

To utilize this power it is important to first understand the **overarching categories of humor.** Then, we will meticulously dissect each of the main categories of humor to equip you with the skills necessary to select and deploy the most suitable plans custom tailored to your unique business, circumstances and goals. We will finish with ways to ensure your marketing is working, and what to do if it's not working.

Table for three please!

When using humor for advertising, we need to rely heavily on **The Rule of Three.** The Rule of Three is a classic principle in storytelling, comedy and humorous writing and is perfect for the requirements of a successful marketing campaign. The Rule of Three says that things presented in threes are inherently funnier, more satisfying, or more effective.

The power of three is why we've recruited a crack team of 3 guides that you can rely on to help you succeed. I've already introduced you to your new BFFs, **Zog, the alien, Byte, the robot**, and **Mr. Coin, the banker**.

Now it's time to start revealing some of the tricks that are used in humor, so that we can get ready to start applying them to our marketing plans. So, let's buckle up for the ride of your marketing life!

Humans are built to recognize patterns.

Three quick elements establish a rhythm and build anticipation, which leads us to a punchline, also known as a climax. Here's a breakdown of how it works:

- **Setup**: Introduces a concept or idea, establishing a pattern. This happens because our brains automatically make assumptions and start to create a story with expectations.

- **Confirmation**: Reinforces the pattern, leading the audience to anticipate a continuation in the next step.

- **Subversion**: Breaks the pattern with an unexpected twist, often leading to the punchline. This final part is crucial as it surprises the audience and triggers laughter or a deeper appreciation of the joke or story.

The Rule of Three works because the human brain is *pattern-seeking* . Once the pattern is established, breaking it creates a surprising or humorous effect. This rule can be seen in classic jokes, storytelling, speeches, and even in visual arts and music. The best ads use them to great effect. It's a testament to the power of this structure in creating engaging and memorable content.

Later on, with **Byte, the robot**, we'll start putting the power of three, along with other humor strategies to work;

but first I want to repeat the important humor elements to reinforce them, so you can start seeing them in action around you. This applies in movies, commercials (I'll break down examples too), and in real life when you or someone near you laughs at something funny.

So sure, we've got a crack team of navigational experts ready to lead you through the wild, and sometimes wacky, world of humor-infused marketing campaigns. But don't be mistaken: Humor in business is serious business[2]. Humor is a competitive advantage that is under-utilized by most marketers. You're probably thinking, wait, I've seen the big guys use humor for years. True! The big guys got big for a reason. They know how to successfully create, deploy and manage humor. Now it's your turn.

So let's get a full understanding of how we can organize and wield the power of humor like a true master of our own universe. The aliens are going to overtake us with laughter not lasers. With **Zog, the alien**, **Byte, the robot**, and **Mr. Coin, the banker** by your side, you will be the winner.

All humor and laughter is based on *surprise* and *misdirection*. It's the unexpected surprise, the break from the norm that gets your heart happy, your belly jiggling and your relationships ready to expand.

---

[2] https://www.gsb.stanford.edu/insights/humor-serious-business

We'll dive deeper into the details of how to use surprise, but we'll start by looking at the categories themselves. **Zog the alien** leads the way to reveal the many categories and the key elements so you gain an understanding of the overarching secrets of humor so you'll know where to get started on a campaign. Why did we recruit an alien as our guide? It's so that you know where to go when you have a new marketing need. Zog the alien turns unknown concepts into categories that are easy to understand, and allows you to pick a direction quickly and easily before getting into the details.

Once we start to understand the landscape, we will then dive into the details, learn the techniques and build funny, memorable marketing plans with **Byte the robot.** Byte will take you into the details, as we meticulously dissect each of the main humor categories to equip you with the skills necessary to understand and deploy effective marketing plans tailored to your unique circumstances.

Finally, **Mr. Coin, the banker** will crunch the numbers and finish with strategies to ensure your marketing is working. If **Mr. Coin** discovers you're not getting proper results, he knows what to do to get you back on track by directing you through your missteps and helps you maneuver through them for positive outcomes.

Your Guides to Marketing With Humor:

- Zog, the alien - Will map out what humor in marketing is. This is an easy place to start.

- Byte, the robot - Navigates the details so you can use humor in your business.

- Mr. Coin, the banker - Helps you decipher what's working or not working, and advises from there.

Step 1 (with Zog) - Observation: We will lay out the best ways to gather information. This is a common technique in humor. This is the planning phase. We start to gather information and list the data for us to assess. This will get us prepared to create. This is gathering the details of what we will play with later. Observation is important because it's the details that later become the relatable moments that grab our attention, build tension, and then break the tension with an outburst of laughter or amusement. We'll get more detailed with Robot as our guide in the next chapter.

Step 2 - Write & Filter (with Byte): The information we've gathered is used to write what will become the subject of our marketing materials. You have to think of this as a mini movie. But it's quick: Bing, bang, boom. Over. Message delivered. The good news is because humor is designed to be short, the process is short too. We're really only going for one joke. We can decide to expand it later into a series of sorts, but for now the goal is one joke.

During the writing and filtering process we will start to see concepts emerge. We want to push ourselves without judgment at the start. For now we're talking about brainstorming sessions so wild it'll be like dancing with wolves like nobody's watching. We start to choose the type of humor in our marketing by running the details of our story through a filtering process to uncover what works best for your business and customers.

Now, brace yourself for the surprise twist! We're flipping the script, turning assumptions on their head, and leaving your audience gasping for air (from laughter, of course). It's like a plot twist in a thriller movie, but way funnier! This is where the twist comes in. From here we continue by playing with different ways of executing the misdirection and surprise.

Step 3 - Create - We'll work with 3 categories of humor we crafted from the best in the business. We choose one or more of what many humorists refer to as "funny filters." This is where the humor starts to come to life, with some testing and refinement to follow. This is the process where you will start to uncover the laughs and humor. It's an eye opening step that opens your mind up to the power and possibilities of humor for your businesses' success.

As stated in the previous chapter, we will rely heavily on The Rule of Three. This will become our shortcut to storytelling and humorous writing for our marketing. This creates the framework for a successful marketing campaign and will make our marketing campaigns inherently funnier, more satisfying, and more effective.

Once we have some solid ideas to work with, we can produce the media and content needed to start building relationships.

Step 4 - Launch - This is where we put the pieces into actual marketing and advertising layouts, specs, and start testing them. As they start to work, we create a feedback loop that ultimately fuels **Mr. Coin the Banker's** tasks of measuring and refining the results, goals and success of the marketing piece you've created.

Every marketer worth their salt should be flexing their funny bone, and every business should know how to serve up laughs with their products and services. When you mix business with humor, the results are nothing short of magical!

And the best part? Adding humor, and using the formulas in this book is not much harder than what you're already doing. It's much less painful to use humor in your marketing than it is to get average results from your marketing efforts. Once you get your brain around the concepts, it's quick, flexible, and heck, it can be more fun than a tire swing on a lake if it's done correctly.

With a little bit of practice, I promise you'll walk away knowing more about one of the most powerful tools in marketing, and how to use more humor to make your business more profitable. Whether you're a marketing maestro or a newbie on the scene, humor is the secret sauce that'll take your business from zero to hero. If you've been at it a while, you'll go from hero to master of the universe.

✔ Bonus Guide:
Humor in Marketing Starter Kit.

Enlist the help of Zog the Alien, Byte the Robot, and Mr. Coin the Banker, with their Starter Kit, Cheat Sheet, and Scorecard.

AlienRobotBanker.com/ToolKit

Ready, set, don't forget...

03

Zog, The Alien

Reveals the
Formulas and Plans

CHAPTER THREE

Zog, The Alien - Reveals the Formulas and Plans

Humor is Power!

Humor isn't just a chuckle; it's a force to be reckoned with. By mastering the secret formulas of humor, you'll be wielding a power so mighty even the Avengers would be impressed. And guess what? You don't need a PhD in comedy, or even to be funny yourself, to get in on the action. Nope, it's possible for anyone to learn the formulas of humor so as to become a master of hilarity in your marketing and your business.

Zog, the alien is your trusty navigator through the cosmos of comedy. Have you ever felt like you're in outer space when it comes to understanding something? Well, humor is no different. So now we'll make a simple and short reference guide. From decoding the different types of humor to breaking down those bizarre concepts, Zog makes sure you're not lost in space. With Zogs help you'll grasp the basics, see the big picture, and be able to pick the path that suits your style. In a world where every website looks like a carbon copy of the next, humor is your secret weapon for grabbing attention, winning hearts, and leaving your competitors in the dust! **Zog, the alien** will start to cover the basics and how you can identify what humor in marketing means to and for your business.

Mastering the secret formulas of humor

This is really about a proven method of marketing that moves you and your business from LOL to ROI: We're mapping out the codes of comedy that many have used to master humor in marketing for business and personal gain.

Humor Types: Introduction

There are different types of humor that can be used for different means. That being said, they mostly fall within the three following sub-categories:

1. Mismatch

2. Misplaced Sincerity

3. Exaggeration (and Absurdity)

The Unexpected

The unexpected is the core of all humor. It takes many forms, but it's the surprise that produces the feeling of fun and excitement. As we go into the details of 1. Mismatch 2. Misplaced Sincerity, and 3. Exaggeration, we'll start to understand how playing with the unexpected allows you to play with your customers in a way that bonds them to your business.

You see, the brain is like a mystery-solving machine, always trying to predict what comes next. But when you flip the script and hit 'em with the unexpected, that's when the magic happens. It's like a punchline that sneaks up and smacks you right in the funny bone! It's our brains' shortcut to problem solving, and it's known as pattern recognition. We humans do it automatically, and we're really good at it.

As you're dishing out info left and right about who, what, when, where, why, and how, your audience isn't waiting for you to tell them every detail. Oh no, they're making assumptions faster than you can say "return on investment".

Broken Assumptions

Every time you speak, you provide the listener with information about the who, what, where, when, why, or how of your story. Everything you say or show leads the audience to assume the rest. This is where the opportunity lies to play with their assumptions. Now is where we start adding the formulas of humor - 1. Mismatch 2. Misplaced Sincerity or, 3. Exaggeration.

Mismatch

In our lives we have hundreds of normal situations everyday. During those situations we behave normally. Mismatch is when you have either:

1. A Normal Behavior occurring during an Abnormal Situation. OR

2. An Abnormal Behavior occurring during a Normal Situation

Here are some examples of funny ads featuring mismatch:

1. **Snickers' "You're Not You When You're Hungry" Series**: One ad features a group of men working on a construction site, but when one of them is hungry, he behaves dramatically like a diva until he eats a Snickers and returns to normal. The normal behavior of eating a snack becomes humorous because of the exaggerated abnormal situation.

2. **Old Spice's "The Man Your Man Could Smell Like" Commercial**: The spokesman engages in normal conversation about body wash, but he does it while rapidly changing locations and settings, from a bathroom to a boat, to a horse. The absurdity of the rapid scene changes makes the normal conversation funny.

3. **Doritos' "Goat 4 Sale" Commercial:** A man buys a goat that loves Doritos. The goat engages in normal eating behavior, but it becomes hilarious when the man discovers the goat's insatiable appetite for Doritos, leading to an unusual and chaotic situation at home.

These examples use the contrast between behavior and situation to create humor and make the advertisements memorable. In Steal Like an Artist by Austin Kleon,[3] he suggests that you write down examples and replace the details with your own details. Now would be a good time to get started. Grab a notepad or open your Google Doc and start compiling a list of ideas you can use for your business's marketing and communications.

Use the lined note pages I've added throughout the book to get you started.

---

[3] Austin Kleon, Steal Like an Artist: 10 Things Nobody Told You About Being Creative

Misplaced Sincerity

Misplaced sincerity in humor involves characters displaying earnestness or seriousness in situations that are absurd, trivial, or inappropriate. This contrast between the character's serious attitude and the ridiculous context creates a comedic effect.

Here are some ways misplaced sincerity is used in humor:

1. **Irony**: Characters take trivial matters very seriously, leading to humorous irony. For example: someone might treat a minor inconvenience, like a broken pencil, as if it were a major life crisis, creating a funny contrast between the situation's actual significance and the character's reaction.

2. **Parody**: Misplaced sincerity is often used in parodies to mock genres, styles, or specific works. A parody of a serious movie genre (like a spy thriller or a medical drama) might feature characters who remain intensely serious even when the situations are blatantly absurd or exaggerated, highlighting the original genre's tendencies.

3. **Deadpan Delivery**: Comedians often use deadpan delivery, where they speak or act with a serious tone and expression while describing or doing something absurd. This delivery style enhances the humor because the audience expects a serious topic but gets something completely ridiculous instead.

4. **Overreaction**: Characters might overreact to small, everyday problems with excessive seriousness, making the situation funnier. For instance a character might organize an elaborate plan to fix a very minor issue, like a small stain on their shirt, treating it as if it were a matter of national security.

5. **Juxtaposition**: Placing a sincerely serious character in a completely inappropriate or mundane setting creates humor through juxtaposition. For example, a character might give a heartfelt motivational speech about something trivial, like organizing their sock drawer, using language and intensity more suitable for a significant life event.

6. **Unexpected Formality**: Misplaced sincerity can also occur when a character uses overly formal language or behavior in casual or inappropriate settings. For example, someone might use flowery, poetic language to describe a simple meal, making the situation humorous because of the mismatch in tone.

7. **Children or Animals**: Using children or animals who speak or act with misplaced sincerity can be especially funny. For example, a child might seriously explain a completely fantastical or nonsensical story as if it were fact, or an animal might be anthropomorphized to express sincere concern over something trivial.

Examples of Misplaced Sincerity outside of marketing:

1. **Ron Burgundy in "Anchorman"**: Ron Burgundy's serious delivery of utterly absurd news stories and his earnest but misplaced confidence in his own importance create a humorous contrast.

2. **Dwight Schrute in "The Office"**: Dwight takes his job and personal missions extremely seriously, even when they are ridiculous or trivial, such as his intense dedication to office safety drills or his exaggerated sense of authority.

3. **"Monty Python and the Holy Grail"**: The knights in this film treat their absurd quests with utmost seriousness. For example, the Black Knight's refusal to admit defeat, even after losing multiple limbs, is funny because of his unwavering sincerity in an obviously hopeless situation.

By presenting sincere behavior in inappropriate or absurd contexts, misplaced sincerity creates a comedic dissonance that surprises and entertains the audience.

Here are some examples of funny advertisements that use misplaced sincerity to create humor:

1. **Terry Tate "Office Linebacker" (Reebok)**: In these ads, Terry Tate is hired as an "office linebacker" to enforce productivity and office rules. His over-the-top enforcement and the seriousness with which he tackles minor office infractions, like not refilling the coffee pot, create a humorous contrast.

2. **Kmart "Ship My Pants"**: This ad features customers seriously discussing how they can "ship" their pants (and other items) for free. The play on words and the characters' earnest tone while saying something that sounds like an inappropriate phrase create a humorous effect.

3. **Budweiser "Whassup?"**: This series of ads features friends greeting each other with exaggerated enthusiasm, saying "Whassup?" in a very serious tone, despite the silliness of the situation. The misplaced sincerity of the greeting becomes the joke.

These ads use misplaced sincerity to create a humorous dissonance, making the audience laugh by presenting serious attitudes in absurd or trivial contexts.

Exaggeration and Absurdity

"Exaggeration" refers to the act of representing something as more extreme or dramatic than it actually is, often in a humorous or ridiculous way. "Absurd" refers to something that is unreasonable, illogical, or contrary to expectations in a humorous or ridiculous way.

To simplify our understanding of **absurdity**, here are some examples of absurd situations:

- A penguin trying to fly an airplane.
- A talking banana attending a job interview.
- A fish riding a bicycle through the desert.
- A cat wearing a top hat and monocle, hosting a tea party for mice.
- A superhero whose only power is the ability to turn invisible in the dark.

To simplify our understanding of **exaggeration**, here are some examples of exaggerated situations:

- A bodybuilder lifting a mountain with one hand.
- A marathon runner finishing a race in the blink of an eye.

- A student studying so hard that their textbooks catch fire.

- A chef cooking a meal so spicy that it melts the kitchen.

- A singer hitting a note so high that it shatters the moon.

- A gardener growing flowers that reach up to the clouds.

- A writer typing so fast that the keyboard starts smoking.

- A dancer spinning so quickly that they create a tornado.

- A football player kicking a ball into space.

- An artist painting a picture so realistic that it comes to life.

This is where you start. Short and simple ideas to get moving in the right direction.

Exaggeration starts with the known and familiar and takes us on a journey to fun, happiness and attachment. Exaggeration is a powerful tool in humor because it amplifies normal characteristics or situations to an extreme, creating a contrast that is often surprising and absurd. This contrast catches the audience off guard and can lead to laughter.

Exaggeration and understatement must have an element of reality to be effective. This is why using specifics from your business is a critical ingredient that allows you to highlight your business and tie everything together.

Here are some examples of funny advertisements that use exaggeration to create humor:

1. **Progressive "Superstore"**: In these ads, the exaggerated setting of an insurance superstore highlights the absurdity of treating insurance shopping like buying groceries. Characters interact with insurance products as if they are tangible items on store shelves, creating a humorous exaggeration of the insurance purchasing process.

2. **Skittles "Taste the Rainbow"**: Many Skittles ads use exaggeration to highlight the candy's flavors. For example, one ad shows a man with the ability to turn everything he touches into Skittles. The exaggerated consequence of this power leads to absurd and humorous situations.

3. **Evian "Baby & Me"**: This ad features adults who see their reflections as babies in a mirror. The exaggerated concept of adults behaving like infants, complete with dancing and playful antics, creates a humorous and charming visual.

It's easy to use at a local level too. Here are some examples of local advertisements that use exaggeration to create humor:

1. **Vern Fonk Insurance**: Based in the Pacific Northwest, Vern Fonk Insurance commercials often feature exaggerated and absurd humor. One memorable ad parodies a famous scene from "The Matrix," with the protagonist choosing Vern Fonk for insurance in a dramatically exaggerated fashion.

2. **J.G. Wentworth "877-CASH-NOW"**: This financial services company, although national, has created many local versions of its famous opera-style commercials. The exaggerated opera singing and dramatic calls for cash now are humorous due to their over-the-top delivery.

3. **Crazy Gideon's Electronics**: A well-known local ad in Los Angeles, Crazy Gideon's commercials feature the owner shouting exaggerated claims about his low prices and wild antics, such as smashing electronics to show his frustration with high prices elsewhere.

These advertisements use exaggeration to create humor by amplifying the enthusiasm, benefits, or scenarios associated with their products or services, making them memorable and entertaining for viewers. Don't just read or skim the examples above, start using them as the framework for your own business marketing campaigns. Replace the situations and details to get you started with your own humorous marketing campaigns.

Pop Culture

I've added Pop Culture because it's another humorous shortcut that helps us create a faster setup. Pop Culture is a catch-all phrase for things we are familiar with. It could be anything from the news to a TikTok trend. This is where we start. It's a short cut to the set up. We'll dive deeper into set up later, but with storytelling in marketing we've got to be quicker than a squirrel on an espresso binge. Short cuts are a big part of what humor in marketing is all about.

In order to get to the unexpected surprise we need for humor in our marketing campaigns, we need to have a roadmap. The roadmap is the process for getting from everyday occurrences to laughing and enjoying those mundane events. This starts with observing what is around us everyday, at work, at home, on vacation, and is commonly known as "observational humor". It's the real world where we will start to play with things that take us to exaggeration and absurdity, leading us ultimately to laughter and connection.

Humor often uses pop culture, clichés, and familiar expressions to create setups faster because these elements are widely recognized and understood by the audience. By leveraging shared knowledge, we can quickly establish context, set up jokes, and deliver punchlines without needing extensive explanations. Here's how each element contributes to this process:

Pop Culture

1. **Instant Recognition**: References to popular movies, TV shows, celebrities, or trends are immediately recognizable. This familiarity allows the audience to quickly grasp the context and background, saving time on setup.

   - **Example**: A commercial might show someone trying to assemble furniture and then cut to a scene mimicking a popular superhero calling for help, playing on the audience's knowledge of superhero tropes to quickly set up a humorous situation.

2. **Shared Experiences**: Pop culture references tap into shared experiences and emotions, creating a sense of camaraderie and understanding between the performer and the audience.

   - **Example**: An ad parodying a well-known movie scene, like the famous "You can't handle the truth!" moment from "A Few Good Men," can immediately evoke recognition and laughter.

Clichés

1. **Predictable Patterns**: Clichés rely on familiar patterns or situations that the audience can anticipate. This predictability allows comedians to subvert expectations, leading to humor.

   - **Example**: A commercial might show a cliché romantic scene with soft music and a sunset, only to have it hilariously interrupted by an unexpected event, like a loud product demonstration.

2. **Shortcut to Concepts**: Clichés act as shortcuts to convey complex ideas or situations quickly. They encapsulate common scenarios or phrases that audiences immediately understand.

   - **Example**: An ad might use the cliché of a used car salesman with exaggerated friendliness and fast-talking, playing on the audience's preconceived notions for comedic effect.

Familiar Expressions

1. **Double Meanings**: Familiar expressions often have well-known meanings, and twisting these meanings can create humor through wordplay or situational irony.

- **Example**: A commercial might take the expression "break the bank" literally, showing someone smashing a piggy bank with a hammer to make a financial point humorously.

1. **Expectation Subversion**: Using a familiar expression and then subverting it in an unexpected way can create surprise and laughter.

    - **Example**: An ad might start with the familiar phrase "As easy as pie," and then show a character struggling hilariously with baking, highlighting the irony.

Combined Effect

1. **Efficient Storytelling**: By combining pop culture, clichés, and familiar expressions, humor can build context and character quickly, allowing more time for the comedic payoff.

    - **Example**: A commercial might feature a character behaving like a cliché action hero (using familiar tropes and expressions) in a mundane setting like an office. The quick setup allows the ad to focus on the humor of the situation.

2. **Audience Engagement**: Recognizable references and expressions engage the audience by making them feel "in on the joke." This shared understanding enhances the comedic impact.

   ▪ **Example**: An ad referencing a current pop culture trend, like a viral dance, can instantly engage viewers who recognize and appreciate the reference, setting up a humorous scenario quickly.

By observing your own business and the daily occurrences there, you'll start to see things that we all understand. These familiar occurrences, clichés and Pop culture references can be combined for a power effect.

Here are some ad examples:

1. **Geico's "Horror Movie Clichés"**: This ad uses the familiar clichés of horror movies (like characters making obviously bad decisions) to set up the humor quickly. The audience immediately recognizes the tropes, allowing the joke to land faster.

2. **State Farm's "Jake from State Farm"**: The ad uses the familiar setup of a late-night phone call and the cliché suspicion of infidelity, only to reveal that the caller is talking to an insurance agent. The quick recognition of the situation sets up the humorous twist.

3. **Old Spice "The Man Your Man Could Smell Like"**: These ads use over-the-top masculinity clichés and pop culture references to create humor. The exaggerated scenarios and familiar tropes quickly set up the joke.

By utilizing pop culture, clichés, and familiar expressions, humor can efficiently establish context, subvert expectations, and deliver punchlines that resonate quickly with the audience.

In the next chapter, Byte, The Robot will show us how to start creating our own versions of these fun formulas.

Here is an outline of what we'll cover.

Step 1 - **Observation**. We gather information to write the script. Jerry Seinfeld says that "everything is material." That's really good news for us because it makes our job easier. We'll start to look at ourselves, our customers, how we do business. It's all fodder for folly.

Step 2 - **Write & Filter**: We write the story as we run the details through the strategies of humor that have been used and proven for a long long time.

Step 3 - **Produce** - Once we have completed the humor steps we will start to produce the media content needed to start connecting with our customers.

Step **4** - **Launch** - This is where we start to see where our humor is connecting with our intended audience. It's all about launching, measuring and making the needed changes for success.

Now it's time to start creating your first success story using humor as a tool to connect with your customers in a more meaningful way, using Zog the alien's layout to get you started. As Zog points out, "Humor isn't just about making people laugh; it's a tool for connection." Now let's join our new robot friend, Byte, to lay out the details of humors' most powerful tool: the unexpected. Your audience is constantly trying to predict what's next. This builds tension and conflict. When you release that tension and disrupt their expectations, that's when the humor happens through using the three key techniques of **Mismatch, Misplaced Sincerity, and Exaggeration.**

Mismatch, where normal behavior occurs in abnormal situations—like a serious business meeting turning into a dance-off. Misplaced Sincerity, where exaggerated politeness or formality is applied in a ridiculous context. And Exaggeration, where absurdity heightens a common situation beyond belief. "Each of these plays with your customers' assumptions. It's that twist they didn't see coming that will bond them to your brand."

With these tools, you're ready to jump into the building process of marketing with a twist and start adding humor to your business with Byte, the robot.

✓ Zog, The Alien's - Starter Kit.

Bonus Guide: Humor in Marketing Starter Kit.

Start here with the help of Zog the Alien to turn the unknown concepts into categories that are easy to understand and allow you to pick a direction quickly and easily before getting into the details.

AlienRobotBanker.com/starterkit

👥🎗 Ready, set, don't forget...

_____

_____

_____

_____

_____

_____

_____

_____

_____

_____

_____

_____

_____

_____

_____

_____

_____

_____

_____

_____

_____

_____

_____

04

Byte, The Robot

Building Humor Formulas for Your Marketing

CHAPTER FOUR

Byte, The Robot - Building Humor Formulas for Your Marketing

To really understand the theory of how best to add humor to your marketing, we'll dive deeper into the details that will help keep us organized and moving toward success.

As we get into the details, you'll want to use these examples and the many others you come across, as inspiration to launch your media and marketing campaigns. "Be curious about the world in which you live. Look things up. Chase down every reference. Go deeper than anybody else--that's how you'll get ahead."[4]

---

[4] — Austin Kleon, Steal Like an Artist: 10 Things Nobody Told You About Being Creative

By now we should be starting to get an understanding of how humor is laid out. It's time to blast off into the specifics. This is where **Byte the Robot** steps in. Byte is your marketing maestro, armed with all the formulas and tricks of the trade used by marketing legends and creative gurus alike. From crafting memorable stories to building your own humor-powered marketing strategy, Byte's got the tools, examples, and worksheets to get you going. As you prepare to sprinkle some humor into your marketing mix, Byte holds the keys to the castle and, if you're willing, he's able to show you the secrets to humor and how to leverage it to succeed in business. It's the one-stop shop you've been dreaming of.

Now get ready to dive headfirst into the wild and wacky world of building humor formulas for your very own business needs! But, remember: You're here to gain an understanding of humor and how it's used in marketing, because then and only then will you be able to use this information successfully.

Step 1 - Observation

Observation: This is where **we gather information** for your marketing campaign using humor.

You have to think of this as a mini movie. It's quick: Bing, bang, boom. Over. Message delivered. So we only need a few things: Subject, character, and location (think one shot).

I want you to grasp onto these concepts quickly and tightly. I use a process known as listing. It's how most successful marketing campaigns that use humor work.

In Jerry Seinfeld's 5-Step Humor Process, Seinfeld says the first thing you have to do is come up with something funny to write about. However, as we already mentioned, everything is material and it's *everywhere*. So, all that we have to do is put them in the right order. The first step is to list them out, and then we can put them in the right order.

Exaggeration and understatement must have a foundation in reality to be effective. Details are crucial in humor to ground them in reality. The details play an important part for several reasons: playing a key role in setting up jokes, enhancing storytelling, and ensuring the punchline lands effectively. These pillars of comedic genius will turn your marketing from meh to memorable!

Here's why the specifics matter so much:

1. **Setting the Scene:** Details help create a vivid, relatable context for the audience. They can transform a generic scenario into something specific and immersive, making the humorous element more impactful by grounding it in a recognizable reality.

2. **Building Anticipation:** The buildup in a joke or humorous story often relies on carefully chosen details to guide the audience's expectations in one direction, only to subvert them with the punchline. This contrast between expectation and reality is a cornerstone of humor.

3. **Enhancing Relatability:** Specific details can make a humorous situation more relatable to the audience. When people recognize elements of their own experiences in a joke or story, they're more likely to find it funny.

4. **Creating Surprises:** Details can introduce elements of surprise or absurdity in a way that broad strokes cannot. By setting up a realistic or relatable scenario with specific details, the sudden introduction of an absurd or unexpected element becomes much funnier.

5. **Supporting Character Development:** In character-based humor, details about a character's personality, quirks, or background can make them more amusing and memorable. These traits can also set up humorous situations that feel true to the character, enhancing the comedy.

6. **Shortcuts:** Use of characters as tropes is similar to how we used Pop Culture earlier. This is a shortcut to the message, a connection and the new relationship and customer. You make a positive impression with your new connection, they find you online and choose your company. If it sounds easy, that's because it is with humor.

7. **Facilitating Wordplay:** Many forms of humor, like puns or double entendres, rely on the nuances of language. Specific details and precise wording are essential to make this type of humor work.

8. **Emphasizing Exaggeration:** We've already touched on this. Exaggeration is a common comedic technique, and details are what make an exaggeration funny rather than unbelievable. By starting with a base of relatable, specific details, the exaggerated elements stand out more starkly and humorously.

Overall, details are not just embellishments in humor; they are fundamental to making jokes land, stories engaging, and comedic concepts come to life. They enable humor to connect with audiences on a personal level, making the funny moments more impactful and memorable.

Using observational humor also involves finding humor in everyday situations, behaviors, and experiences that are familiar to a wide audience. For example, here are some rules and tips to get started with observational humor:

Rules for Observational Humor

1. **Be Authentic**: Talk about things you genuinely find funny or interesting. Authenticity resonates with audiences and makes your humor more relatable. Don't start by being too funny. The fun and humor will come by executing the humor formulas.

2. **Find Common Ground**: Focus on universal experiences that most people can relate to, such as daily routines, common annoyances, or typical human behaviors.

3. **Keep it Simple**: Observational humor works best when it's straightforward. Avoid overcomplicating your observations with too much detail or obscure references.

4. **Highlight the Absurd**: Look for the absurdity in mundane situations. Pointing out the ridiculousness of everyday life can be very funny.

5. **Use Personal Experiences**: Draw from your own life. Personal anecdotes can add a unique and relatable touch to your humor.

6. **Stay Positive**: While it's okay to point out flaws or annoyances, keep the tone light-hearted and avoid being overly negative or mean-spirited.

Where do you get started? Observation can start anywhere. Just start looking around. Here are some areas to observe and use as humor for your business.

1. Daily Routines

- Getting ready in the morning
- Commuting to work or school
- Grocery shopping experiences
- Cooking and eating meals
- Cleaning and household chores

2. Technology

- Smartphone and social media usage
- Virtual meetings and online work
- Common tech issues (Wi-Fi problems, autocorrect mistakes)
- Gadgets and their quirks

3. Relationships

- Interactions with family members
- Dynamics between friends
- Romantic relationships and dating
- Workplace relationships

4. Social Behavior

- Small talk and social niceties
- Public transportation etiquette
- Gym habits and behaviors
- Dining out experiences

5. Cultural Norms

- Holiday traditions and rituals
- Fashion trends and clothing mishaps
- Common phrases and expressions
- Popular hobbies and interests

6. Consumer Experiences

- Shopping habits and retail experiences
- Customer service interactions
- Advertising and marketing clichés
- Product reviews and unboxing experiences

7. Health and Fitness

- Dieting and eating habits
- Exercise routines and gym culture
- Doctor visits and medical experiences
- Sleep patterns and struggles

8. Travel and Transportation

- Airport and airplane experiences
- Road trips and driving quirks
- Hotel stays and accommodations
- Public transportation adventures

9. Weather and Seasons

- Seasonal changes and activities
- Weather-related inconveniences
- Holiday and vacation plans
- Outdoor activities and mishaps

10. Pet Peeves

- Common annoyances (e.g., loud chewing, slow walkers)
- Office pet peeves (e.g., coworkers' habits)
- Customer service frustrations
- Everyday irritations (e.g., traffic, waiting in line)

Example Observations

1. **Daily Routines**: "Why is it that the snooze button only gives you nine more minutes of sleep? Like, who decided nine minutes was the perfect amount of extra sleep?"

2. **Technology**: "Autocorrect is like a really bad friend who doesn't know when to stop making suggestions. 'I didn't mean ducking, but thanks for trying to keep it clean.'"

3. **Relationships**: "Why do we always lie about our interests on first dates? 'Oh, you love hiking? Me too!' when the closest we get to hiking is walking to the fridge."

4. **Social Behavior**: "Isn't it funny how we all pretend to be asleep on public transport just to avoid giving up our seat? Like, 'Nope, I'm in a deep, deep coma right now.'"

5. **Cultural Norms**: "Holiday family gatherings are like a reality show where everyone has a role. There's

> always the drama queen, the peacemaker, and the one who just stirs the pot for fun."

By observing these everyday situations and finding the humor in them, you can create relatable and funny content that resonates with a wide audience. Practice observing and writing down the quirks and absurdities of daily life, and soon you'll find a wealth of material for your observational humor.

Now, we decide on how we'll deliver the script.

Step 2 - Write and Filter

Write. This is where we write the **script.** You have to think of this as a mini movie. But once again, it's quick. Bing, bang, boom. Over. Message delivered.

The good news is, humor is designed to be short. We're really only going for one joke. We can decide to expand it later but for now the number is one.

Collaborate with humor experts: If you're not confident in your ability to be funny, collaborate with humor experts like comedians or writers who can help you develop funny content. Text them with the knowledge you've gained in this book and let them work their magic.

Now we're back to our Humor Types:

1. Mismatch
2. Misplaced Sincerity

3.   Exaggeration

Mismatch:

Writing a funny advertisement using mismatch involves creating humor through unexpected combinations or contrasts. Here's a step-by-step guide to help you craft an ad using mismatch effectively:

1. Identify Your Product or Service

- **Define the Key Benefits**: Understand the main features and benefits of your product or service.

- **Target Audience**: Know your audience's preferences, humor style, and what resonates with them.

2. Choose a Mismatch Concept

- **Contrast**: Select two contrasting elements, such as high vs. low, serious vs. silly, modern vs. old-fashioned, slow vs. fast, big vs. small, the list could go forever. Look around your business for more details and ideas.

- **Unexpected Combinations**: Think of unlikely pairings that create surprise or absurdity.

3. Develop the Scenario

- **Set Up the Context**: Establish a familiar situation where the mismatch will be introduced.

- **Introduce the Mismatch**: Bring in the contrasting element in an unexpected way.

4. Write the Script

- **Opening Hook**: Grab attention with an intriguing or surprising opening that hints at the mismatch.

- **Build Up**: Create a buildup that emphasizes the normalcy of the situation before introducing the mismatch.

- **Punchline**: Deliver the punchline with the unexpected element, making sure it highlights the key benefit of your product or service.

5. Visualize the Ad

- **Storyboarding**: Sketch out key scenes to visualize how the mismatch will be presented.

- **Characters and Setting**: Choose characters and settings that enhance the humor of the mismatch.

- **Timing and Delivery**: Ensure comedic timing and delivery are spot-on to maximize the humor.

Example Ad Using Mismatch

Product: A high-tech fitness tracker.

Mismatch Concept: Medieval knights using a high-tech fitness tracker during training.

Script

Opening Hook (Scene: A medieval battlefield. Knights are preparing for a battle with serious expressions.)

Narrator: "In a time of epic battles and noble quests..."

Build Up (The camera zooms in on Sir Reginald, a knight in full armor. He's stretching and preparing for a joust. Suddenly, he lifts his arm to reveal a modern fitness tracker.)

Sir Reginald: (speaking to another knight) "I've logged 10,000 steps already today, and it's not even noon!"

Introduce the Mismatch (The other knight looks puzzled. Cut to Sir Reginald checking his tracker for his heart rate.)

Sir Reginald: "Look at that heart rate! Perfect for optimal jousting performance."

Punchline (Cut to a close-up of the fitness tracker displaying various stats. Sir Reginald charges into battle, but the scene shifts to him running on a treadmill in a modern gym, still in full armor.)

Narrator: "Track your fitness, no matter the century."

Closing (Scene: Sir Reginald triumphantly holding up his fitness tracker.)

Narrator: "The [Brand] Fitness Tracker – for the modern-day warrior in all of us."

Call to Action (Text on screen with product image) "Get yours today at [website]!"

Tips for Writing Mismatch Ads

1. **Keep It Relatable**: Ensure the normal part of the scenario is something your audience can relate to.

2. **Exaggerate the Contrast**: Make the mismatch as exaggerated as possible to enhance the humor.

3. **Visual and Verbal Balance**: Use both visual gags and dialogue to convey the mismatch effectively.

4. **Test the Concept**: Try out the concept with a sample audience to see if the humor lands as intended.

5. **Stay True to the Brand**: Ensure the humor aligns with your brand's voice and values.

By using mismatch in your advertising, you can create memorable, funny ads that capture attention and make a lasting impression on your audience.

Misplaced Sincerity:

Writing a funny advertisement using misplaced sincerity involves creating humor by placing exaggerated seriousness in trivial or absurd situations. Here's a step-by-step guide to help you craft an ad with misplaced sincerity effectively:

1. Identify Your Product or Service

- **Define the Key Benefits**: Understand the main features and benefits of your product or service.

- **Target Audience**: Know your audience's preferences, humor style, and what resonates with them.

2. Choose the Scenario

- **Trivial Situation**: Select a trivial or mundane situation where misplaced sincerity will be applied.

- **Absurd Elements**: Consider introducing absurd elements to enhance the humor.

3. Develop the Characters

- **Sincere Character**: Create a character who will deliver the misplaced sincerity with complete earnestness. Don't overthink it. Use characters that we are familiar with.

- **Supportive Characters**: Add characters who react to the sincerity in a way that enhances the humor. Add the supporting characters that compliment or contrast the characters and contribute to the story.

4. Write the Script

- **Opening Hook**: Start with a mundane situation that everyone can relate to.

- **Sincere Delivery**: Have the main character deliver their lines with utmost sincerity, despite the triviality of the situation.

- **Punchline and Resolution**: Deliver the punchline by highlighting the contrast between the character's sincerity and the absurdity or triviality of the situation.

5. Visualize the Ad

- **Storyboarding**: Sketch out key scenes to visualize how the misplaced sincerity will be presented.

- **Characters and Setting**: Choose characters and settings that enhance the humor of the misplaced sincerity.

- **Timing and Delivery**: Ensure comedic timing and delivery are spot-on to maximize the humor.

Example Ad Using Misplaced Sincerity

Product: A premium brand of tissues.

Script

Opening Hook (Scene: A bright, sunny park. Families are picnicking, children are playing. The camera zooms in on a middle-aged man, John, sitting on a bench with a box of tissues on his lap.)

Narrator: "In the midst of life's simplest moments..."

Sincere Delivery (John looks solemnly at the camera, holding up a tissue with great reverence.)

John: "There are times when you need more than just a tissue. You need a companion. A confidant. Something that understands the weight of your sneeze and the gravity of your tears."

Building the Sincerity (The camera pans to John gently dabbing his eyes and then wiping his nose with exaggerated care and tenderness.)

John: "This isn't just a piece of paper. It's a testament to craftsmanship. A blend of strength and softness that cradles your nostrils with the care they deserve."

Punchline and Resolution (A child runs by, trips, and falls. John rushes over, kneels down, and solemnly offers the child a tissue, as if it's a priceless gift. The child takes it, bewildered.)

Narrator: "For those moments that demand unparalleled sincerity…"

Closing (Scene: John standing up, holding the tissue box high, the sun shining behind him like a halo.)

Narrator: "[Brand] Tissues – Because every sneeze deserves respect."

Call to Action (Text on screen with product image) "Show your nostrils some love. Visit [website] today!"

Tips for Writing Misplaced Sincerity Ads

1. **Exaggerate the Seriousness**: Ensure the main character's seriousness is over-the-top to highlight the humor.

2. **Relatable Mundane Situations**: Choose situations that are universally relatable but inherently trivial.

3. **Straight-Faced Delivery**: Characters should deliver their lines without any hint of irony or humor.

4. **Supportive Reactions**: Other characters should either play along with the seriousness or react in a way that underscores the absurdity.

5. **Balance Sincerity and Absurdity**: Ensure there is a clear contrast between the character's sincerity and the triviality or absurdity of the situation.

By using misplaced sincerity, you can create humorous advertisements that capture attention and leave a lasting impression on your audience.

Exaggeration:

Writing a funny advertisement using exaggeration involves amplifying features, situations, or behaviors to ridiculous levels to create humor. Here's a step-by-step guide to help you craft an ad with effective exaggeration:

1. Identify Your Product or Service

- **Define the Key Benefits**: Understand the main features and benefits of your product or service.

- **Target Audience**: Know your audience's preferences, humor style, and what resonates with them.

2. Choose the Exaggeration Angle

- **Feature Amplification**: Exaggerate a specific feature or benefit of your product.

- **Situation Overstatement**: Create a scenario where the product's impact is taken to an extreme.

- **Behavioral Hyperbole**: Showcase characters reacting in over-the-top ways to the product.

3. Develop the Scenario

- **Simple Premise**: Start with a simple, relatable premise that can be blown out of proportion.

- **Exaggerated Elements**: Identify elements within the premise that can be exaggerated for comedic effect.

4. Write the Script

- **Opening Hook**: Start with a normal situation that the audience can relate to.

- **Introduce Exaggeration**: Gradually introduce exaggerated elements to build the humor.

- **Punchline and Climax**: Deliver the punchline with maximum exaggeration to create a memorable impact.

5. Visualize the Ad

- **Storyboarding**: Sketch out key scenes to visualize how the exaggeration will be presented.

- **Characters and Setting**: Choose characters and settings that will enhance the humor of the exaggerated elements.

- **Timing and Delivery**: Ensure comedic timing and delivery are spot-on to maximize the humor.

Example Ad Using Exaggeration

Product: A new brand of energy drink.

Script

Opening Hook (Scene: An office setting. Employees are sluggish, yawning, and looking at the clock.)

Narrator: "Feeling the afternoon slump?"

Introduce Exaggeration (Cut to a man, Jake, who opens a can of the energy drink and takes a sip. Suddenly, his eyes widen, and he starts to vibrate slightly.)

Jake: "Wow, that's powerful!"

Building the Exaggeration (Jake starts typing furiously at his computer, finishing an entire day's work in seconds. He then sprints to the copier, making copies at lightning speed. Colleagues watch in astonishment.)

Narrator: "Introducing [Brand] Energy Drink – The ultimate boost to power through your day!"

Climax and Punchline (Jake's productivity escalates absurdly: he fixes the printer, reorganizes the office supplies, and even repaints the office walls in record time. He then zooms out of the office and is seen jogging up a mountain, still holding the can.)

Narrator: "Packed with the energy to conquer anything!"

Closing (Scene: Jake standing triumphantly on top of the mountain, with an eagle perched on his shoulder.)

Narrator: "[Brand] Energy Drink – For when you need to go above and beyond. And then some."

Call to Action (Text on screen with product image) "Get your boost at [website] today!"

Tips for Writing Exaggeration Ads

1. **Identify Key Features to Exaggerate**: Focus on one or two key features or benefits of your product that can be blown out of proportion.

2. **Use Visual and Verbal Exaggeration**: Combine visual gags with exaggerated dialogue or narration to enhance the humor.

3. **Ensure Relatability**: Start with a relatable situation before introducing the exaggerated elements.

4. **Maintain a Logical Flow**: Even though you're exaggerating, the ad should have a logical progression to maintain audience engagement.

5. **Balance Exaggeration with Reality**: While exaggeration is key, make sure there's a balance so that the humor is clear and not confusing.

By using exaggeration, you can create humorous advertisements that are memorable, engaging, and highlight the benefits of your product in a fun and entertaining way.

Step 3 - Test then Create

Congratulations. Most of the work is done. Now it's time to create. But first we will want to test to get an idea of what will work with your audience. Testing advertising concepts to see if they work can be done quickly, easily, and inexpensively using various methods. Here are some effective strategies:

1. Online Surveys and Polls

- **Platforms**: Use tools like SurveyMonkey, Google Forms, or social media polls.

- **Target Audience**: Share your survey with your target audience to gather their opinions on your ad concepts.

- **Feedback**: Ask specific questions about their reactions, what they found funny, and any suggestions for improvement.

2. Focus Groups

- **Small Groups**: Gather a small group of people from your target audience.

- **Discussion**: Present your ad concepts and facilitate a discussion to gauge their reactions and feedback.

- **Inexpensive**: Conduct these sessions in informal settings, like a coffee shop or virtually via Zoom.

3. Social Media Testing

- **Platforms**: Use Facebook, Instagram, or Twitter to share different versions of your ad concepts.

- **Engagement Metrics**: Track likes, shares, comments, and overall engagement to determine which concept resonates most with your audience.

- **A/B Testing**: Run A/B tests by posting two different versions of the ad and comparing the performance.

4. Email Campaigns

- **Newsletter**: Include your ad concepts in your email newsletters and ask for feedback.

- **Direct Response**: Encourage recipients to reply with their thoughts or fill out a short survey.

- **Open Rates and Click-Through Rates**: Monitor these metrics to see which concepts drive more engagement.

5. Landing Pages

- **Dedicated Pages**: Create simple landing pages for each ad concept.

- **Traffic**: Drive traffic to these pages through social media, email campaigns, or PPC ads.

- **Conversion Rates**: Measure which landing page gets more sign-ups, downloads, or other conversions.

6. In-Person Feedback

- **Pop-Up Booths**: Set up a booth in a high-traffic area (like a mall or a community event) and show your ad concepts to passersby.

- **Immediate Reactions**: Ask for immediate feedback and observe reactions.

- **Inexpensive Incentives**: Offer small incentives, like discounts or freebies, for their time and feedback.

7. Online Communities and Forums

- **Relevant Groups**: Share your ad concepts in relevant online communities or forums (e.g., Reddit, niche Facebook groups).

- **Discussions**: Engage with the community and ask for their opinions.

- **Monitor Responses**: Analyze the comments and feedback to see which concept is more popular.

8. Prototypes and Mockups

- **Simple Tools**: Use tools like Canva, Adobe Spark, or even PowerPoint to create mockups of your ads.

- **Feedback Platforms**: Share these mockups on platforms like Behance or Dribble to get feedback from the creative community.

- **Iterate**: Use the feedback to make quick adjustments and improvements.

9. User Testing Services

- **Platforms**: Use services like UserTesting or UsabilityHub.

- **Audience**: Select participants that match your target demographic.

- **Insights**: Gain detailed insights into their reactions and suggestions.

10. Guerrilla Testing

- **Unconventional Methods**: Use quick, creative methods like sidewalk chalkboards with your ad concept, or flyers in coffee shops with tear-off feedback slips.

- **Observation**: Observe reactions and collect feedback in real-time.

Example Process:

1. **Create Mockups**: Design simple mockups of your ad concepts using free tools like Canva.

2. **Run Social Media Polls**: Post the mockups on your social media channels and run a poll to see which concept is preferred.

3. **Send Email Survey**: Include the ad concepts in your next email newsletter with a link to a short survey.

4. **Conduct Focus Groups**: Gather a small group of friends or colleagues who match your target demographic and discuss the ad concepts.

5. **Monitor Engagement**: Track the engagement metrics from social media and email campaigns to determine which concept performs best.

By using these quick, easy, and inexpensive methods, you can gather valuable feedback on your advertising concepts and make informed decisions before investing in a full-scale ad campaign.

Step 4 - Launch and Learn

One step, two step, three step…And finally, the **PAYOFF**: You've earned your audience's trust.

Now, there are a few steps to follow *before* the launch.

The first step is to pick the platform we are going to use.

There are many types of advertising platforms that businesses use to reach their audience, each with its own strengths and applications:

1. Digital Advertising Platforms

- Social Media: Platforms like Facebook, Instagram, Twitter, and LinkedIn offer targeted advertising options based on user demographics, interests, and behaviors.

- Search Engines: Google Ads and Bing Ads are prominent platforms where businesses can place ads on search engine results pages (SERPs) based on keywords.
- Display Networks: These include a range of websites that show ads in the form of banners or small boxes on web pages.

2. Television Advertising

- Traditional TV advertising remains a powerful medium due to its vast reach and the ability to impact a broad audience with high-quality visuals and sound.

3. Radio Advertising

- This includes traditional AM/FM stations as well as digital options like satellite radio and streaming platforms such as Spotify and Pandora.

4. Print Advertising

- Newspapers and magazines are traditional platforms that, despite a decline in print media consumption, still hold value in certain demographics and regions.

5. Outdoor Advertising

- Billboards, bus stops, and other forms of outdoor ads continue to be effective for local advertising and brand visibility in specific geographic areas.

6. Direct Mail Advertising

- Sending promotional materials directly to the homes of potential customers through postal mail can be very effective, particularly for local businesses and targeted promotions.

7. Mobile Advertising

- This includes ads on mobile apps and websites optimized for mobile devices. With the increasing use of smartphones, mobile advertising allows businesses to reach consumers on the go.

8. Online Video Platforms

- Platforms like YouTube provide opportunities for video ads, which can be highly engaging and offer significant creative freedom to showcase products or services.

Each platform has its own set of advantages, and the choice of platform usually depends on the target audience, budget, campaign goals, and content type. Businesses often use a combination of these platforms to achieve the best results in their marketing efforts.

✅ Byte the Robot - Cheat Sheet..

Get examples and insights on how to use the concepts in the book to create better marketing campaigns by using the formulas and strategies of Humor in Marketing.

AlienRobotBanker.com/cheatsheet

Ready, set, don't forget...

05

Mr. Coin, The Banker

How Does
This Measure Up?

CHAPTER FIVE

Mr. Coin, The Banker - How Does this Measure Up?

Can and should we measure everything? Visualize this: I'm chatting with a business buddy about the juicy details of this book. I'm all hyped up, explaining why injecting humor into businesses is like adding sprinkles to ice cream—essential and delightful! Now, my pal, let's call her "Ms. Metrics," she's the big cheese handling those hefty marketing budgets. And boy, does she love her numbers!

She starts firing off questions faster than a caffeinated cheetah on a treadmill. "What about the numbers? The results? The metrics?" Metrics, metrics, and more metrics! It's like she's got a secret crush on spreadsheets.

But here's the scoop: metrics can be as tempting as a chocolate fountain at a wedding. Easy to dive into, but too much can leave you feeling queasy. I've heard it a million times: "Show me the metrics!"

So, as I'm regaling Ms. Metrics with tales of how humor can turn a business from drab to fab, something clicks. It's like watching a light bulb flicker to life above her head. Suddenly, she's nodding along like a bobblehead on a bumpy road.

I dish out examples like candy at Halloween, showing how a dash of humor can work wonders—boosting sales, snagging a spot in customers' hearts, and making competitors green with envy.

Because let's face it, marketing without a sprinkle of humor is like trying to sell tickets to a blockbuster movie without even showing a trailer. You gotta earn people's trust. You gotta earn the right to tell your story. And what better way to do that than with a hearty dose of laughter?

We can't avoid metrics entirely. We just have to make sure we understand the process. Here are some of the best ways to gauge the impact:

1. Engagement Metrics

- **Social Media**: Track likes, shares, comments, and overall engagement on platforms like Facebook,

Instagram, Twitter, and TikTok. High engagement often indicates that the humor resonates with your audience.

- **Video Views and Watch Time**: For video ads, monitor the number of views and the average watch time. A high completion rate suggests that viewers are entertained and engaged.

2. Conversion Rates

- **Sales and Leads**: Measure the increase in sales or leads generated during and after the campaign. Compare these numbers to previous campaigns without humor to assess the impact.

- **Call to Action (CTA) Performance**: Track the click-through rates (CTR) on your CTAs. A humorous ad that captures attention should lead to higher CTRs.

3. Brand Awareness and Recall

- **Surveys and Polls**: Conduct pre- and post-campaign surveys to measure changes in brand awareness and recall. Ask respondents if they remember your ad and what they remember about it.

- **Brand Mentions**: Monitor the increase in online mentions of your brand across social media, forums, and blogs. Positive mentions can indicate successful humor integration.

4. Website Analytics

- **Traffic**: Track the increase in website traffic during and after the campaign. Use tools like Google Analytics to see if visitors are coming from your humorous ads.

- **Behavior Flow**: Analyze how visitors interact with your site. Look for an increase in time spent on your site and a decrease in bounce rates, indicating that the humor kept them engaged.

5. Customer Feedback

- **Reviews and Testimonials**: Collect and analyze customer reviews and testimonials. Positive comments about the ad's humor can indicate its effectiveness.

- **Focus Groups**: Conduct focus groups to get in-depth feedback on the humorous elements of your campaign. Understand what worked and what didn't.

6. Competitive Analysis

- **Benchmarking**: Compare your campaign's performance against competitors' campaigns. Look at similar humorous campaigns in your industry and analyze their effectiveness.

- **Market Share**: Measure any changes in market share that coincide with the timing of your humorous campaign.

7. Sentiment Analysis

- **Social Listening Tools**: Use tools like Brandwatch, Sprout Social, or Hootsuite to analyze the sentiment of online conversations about your brand. Positive sentiment can indicate that the humor was well-received.

- **Content Analysis**: Review the tone of comments and feedback on your ads. Positive and humorous responses suggest that the humor resonated well with your audience.

8. Ad Performance Metrics

- **Cost Per Click (CPC) and Cost Per Acquisition (CPA)**: Monitor CPC and CPA to see if they decrease with the humorous ad, indicating better performance and engagement.

- **Return on Investment (ROI)**: Calculate the ROI of your campaign. A successful humorous campaign should yield a higher ROI compared to non-humorous campaigns.

Here is a framework to get your started, but remember that this is a fluid process that will evolve over time. The goal is to get indications that you're going in the right direction. Don't get trapped here. Just like the process of adding humor to your marketing plans and your business, it's about creating relationships with your audience. Total numbers are not the outcome you're looking for.

Better relationships are. And let's face it. Not everyone will qualify to do business with you. But the ones who do will pay more, and they will pay more often. That's a loyal customer. The 80/20 rule states that these types of customers are the ones who keep your business growing and thriving.

Example Process:

1. **Launch Campaign**: Introduce the humorous campaign across various channels (social media, email, video platforms).

2. **Track Engagement**: Use social media analytics to track likes, shares, comments, and views.

3. **Monitor Website Traffic**: Check Google Analytics for changes in website traffic and behavior flow.

4. **Collect Feedback**: Conduct surveys and focus groups to gather qualitative feedback on the ad's humor.

5. **Analyze Sales Data**: Compare sales data before, during, and after the campaign.

6. **Sentiment Analysis**: Use social listening tools to measure sentiment and monitor brand mentions.

7. **Compare Metrics**: Benchmark against previous non-humorous campaigns and competitors' campaigns.

8. **Adjust and Optimize**: Use the insights to tweak future campaigns for better performance.

As Mr. Coin would say, metrics are your compass, but they're not the entire map. The key isn't just to collect data but to interpret it wisely. Humor can deepen relationships and build loyalty, but you need to gauge its effectiveness through thoughtful metrics like engagement, conversions, and customer sentiment. Don't let the numbers overshadow the goal: creating genuine connections with your audience. When done right, humor and metrics work hand-in-hand to drive long-term business success, and as Mr. Coin would remind us—those loyal, laughing customers are your most valuable asset.

By combining these methods, you can comprehensively measure the effectiveness of adding humor to your marketing campaigns and make informed decisions for future strategies.

✔ Mr. Coin the Banker - Scorecard

See how things add up and contribute to your bottom line in your marketing. Rate your results, keep and amplify what is working, and boot the rest!

AlienRobotBanker.com/scorecard

Ready, set, don't forget...

06

Next Steps

CHAPTER SIX

Next Steps

M ost marketing campaigns fail to pay off or produce only mediocre results. We want more as marketers and business owners. Adding humor is the tool that offers real connection and brand loyalty, which leads to more sales, better reviews, and bigger bank accounts. By mastering the secret formulas of humor you'll be wielding a powerful marketing and business tool. Formulas are the secret sauce to unlocking this powerful force. These tricks of the trade are learnable and will propel your business forward into new and exciting places, making your bank account, and the world, a richer place.

Now let's jump into a quick recap of what we learned and how to get started. We can't do everything we learned all at once and it will take some time to feel comfortable with these formulas and techniques. Taking small actionable steps is how we're going to do it.

The unexpected is at the core of all humor. It takes many forms but it's the setup that creates an expectation and misdirection creates the surprise that produces the release, fun and connection. It's this release that creates the feeling of connection and delivers entertainment and appreciation from your audience.

Humor Types: RECAP

1. Mismatch - Writing a funny advertisement using mismatch involves creating humor through unexpected combinations or contrasts.

2. Misplaced Sincerity in humor involves characters displaying earnestness or seriousness in situations that are absurd, trivial, or out of place. This contrast between the character's serious attitude and the ridiculous context creates a comedic effect.

3. Exaggeration (and Absurdity) - Writing a funny advertisement using exaggeration involves amplifying features, situations, or behaviors to ridiculous levels to create humor. Heightening through the power of three is how we get there.

The Unexpected.

The unexpected is at the core of all humor. It's the experience of surprise that causes us to feel good about ourselves and your brand. We take advantage of the fact that the brain is like a mystery-solving machine, always trying to predict what comes next. It's the flip of the script and the unexpected that creates the magic.

Broken Assumptions

Saying the what, who, where, when, why, or how is how we start to play with our observations to create the unexpected. Playing with the details in your advertising is key to adding humor and creating that connection. Everything you say or show leads the audience to assume the rest. With the formulas of humor (1. Mismatch, 2. Misplaced Sincerity or 3. Exaggeration) and some practice, you'll be on your way.

Pop Culture and Cliches.

Pop Culture references are how we speed up the process. **Pop Culture helps us get Instant Recognition**, and connect with **Shared Experiences**: Pop culture references tap into shared experiences and emotions, creating a sense of camaraderie and understanding between the performer and the audience.

Clichés rely on familiar patterns or situations that the audience can anticipate. This predictability allows comedians to subvert expectations, leading to humor.

FamiliarExpressions often have well-known meanings, and twisting these meanings creates humor.

By utilizing pop culture, clichés, and familiar expressions, humor can efficiently establish context, subvert expectations, and deliver punchlines that resonate quickly and effectively with the audience.

What if it's not a funny business? What if it's a serious business?

If your business is about as funny as a tax audit—Don't sweat it! Even the most serious businesses can get a chuckle or two. Just ask Geico—the Government Employees Insurance Company—whose fate took a wild turn when they introduced that snazzy gecko. That little lizard didn't just change the insurance game; it turned Warren Buffet into a smiling billionaire! Now, if that's not a punchline waiting to happen, I don't know what is.

These days, humor is not just sprinkled here and there; it's slathered on thicker than peanut butter on a sandwich. It's like our earliest form of social currency— babies have been cracking up since day one! When we laugh, we're basically shouting to the world, "Hey, I like you!"

Take TikTok, for example. It's like a comedy club on steroids! People can't get enough of those goofy videos, and neither can your potential customers. Heck, humor is not just a magic trick; it's a skill you can learn faster than mastering the perfect selfie angle. OK, maybe not quite that fast. But definitely faster than most people think. Not 10,000 hours. We're talking weeks or even days if you're ambitious and focused.

✓ Bonus Guide: Humor in Marketing Tool Kit.

Enlist the help of Zog the Alien, Byte the Robot, and Mr. Coin the Banker, with their Starter Kit, Cheat Sheet, and Scorecard.

AlienRobotBanker.com/ToolKit

Ready, set, don't forget...

Bonus Chapter:
Funny Bone

Bonus Chapter: Funny Bone

Where's my funny bone?

Imagine you're in a doctor's office, standing next to an x-ray machine. The doctor, with a curious look, suggests taking a scan to find your elusive "funny bone." You step under the machine, and the x-ray hums to life, its light tracing the contours of your skeleton. The doctor examines the images with a furrowed brow.

"Interesting," the doctor muses. "There's no sign of a funny bone anywhere in your body."

You're puzzled, thinking this confirms what you've always believed—that humor is something you're born with. That not everyone has the ability to be funny. But then, the doctor switches to another scan, this time focusing on your brain. The screen lights up, revealing something unexpected.

"Look here," the doctor points to a bright spot in your brain. "This is where your humor resides."

You see the vibrant, glowing area, representing creativity, wit, and the ability to see the lighter side of life. It's not a physical bone but a mental spark, a neural network that lights up with every joke, every playful thought.

The metaphor here is clear: searching for your funny bone with an x-ray machine only reveals that humor isn't a tangible part of your body; it's an intrinsic part of your mind.

It's not about possessing a physical attribute but nurturing a mental state. Your brain, with its complex web of neurons, holds the key to your sense of humor and everyone has it. It's a reminder that humor is cultivated through perspective, imagination, and the willingness to find and nurture this joy in everyday life.

Resources and Tools: Here is a list of books that will help you dive deeper into humor. They expand and dive deeper into the categories of humor for a more in depth understanding. These are my favorite books about humor, each with a brief summary to help you decide which ones are best for you on your journey.

1. *The Comedy Bible: From Stand-up to Sitcom–The Comedy Writer's Ultimate Guide* by Judy Carter

   Summary: This comprehensive guide by Judy Carter covers various aspects of writing and performing comedy. The book provides step-by-step instructions on creating stand-up routines, writing sitcom scripts, and understanding comedic timing. Carter also offers practical exercises and tips to help aspiring comedians develop their unique comedic voice and style.

2. *Born Standing Up: A Comic's Life* by Steve Martin

   Summary: Although primarily a memoir, Steve Martin's book offers valuable insights into the world of stand-up comedy and the process of developing humor. Martin shares his journey from a young magician to a successful comedian, providing tips on writing jokes, crafting performances, and connecting with audiences. It's a blend of personal anecdotes and practical advice for anyone interested in comedy.

3. *The Comic Toolbox: How to Be Funny Even If You're Not* by John Vorhaus

    Summary: John Vorhaus's book is a practical guide to writing humor for various formats, including sitcoms, novels, and stand-up. The book covers fundamental principles of comedy, such as the rule of three, exaggeration, and reversals. Vorhaus offers exercises and examples to help readers practice and refine their comedic writing skills.

4. *Truth in Comedy: The Manual of Improvisation* by Charna Halpern, Del Close, and Kim Howard Johnson

    Summary: This book focuses on the principles of improvisational comedy, emphasizing the importance of truth and authenticity in creating humor. The authors, who are pioneers in improv, provide techniques and exercises to help performers develop their improvisational skills. The book is valuable for anyone looking to enhance their spontaneity and creativity.

5. *Writing Comedy for Television* by Ronald Wolfe

Summary: Ronald Wolfe's book is a detailed guide to writing comedy for TV. It covers the structure of sitcoms, character development, dialogue writing, and the intricacies of crafting comedic scenes. Wolfe draws on his extensive experience in the industry to provide practical tips and examples, making this a useful resource for aspiring television writers.

6. *Humor That Works: The Missing Skill for Success and Happiness at Work* by Andrew Tarvin

Summary: Andrew Tarvin's book explores how humor can be a valuable tool in the workplace. He provides practical advice on using humor to improve communication, enhance creativity, and boost employee engagement. The book includes exercises and strategies for incorporating humor into professional settings, making it accessible and relevant for a business audience.

✔ Bonus Guide: Humor Kit.

Enlist the help of Zog the Alien, Byte the Robot, and
Mr. Coin the Banker, with their Cheat Sheet, Starter
Kit, and Scorecard.

AlienRobotBanker.com/ToolKit

Ready, set, don't forget...

_____

_____

_____

_____

_____

_____

_____

_____

_____

_____

_____

_____

_____

_____

_____

_____

_____

_____

_____

Conclusion

Conclusion

As you close this book, remember that the future of business is in your hands. Dare to innovate, challenge the status quo, and create a legacy that will inspire generations to come. The journey is just beginning, and the world is waiting for your impact.

I'll never forget the moment when I realized that adding humor is not about being the funniest person around but about truly caring about my customers enough to go the extra millimeter or mile to make the business and the lives of those I serve better. And in the process add some dollars to my bank account. The insight and success I've experienced by adding humor has transformed my career and can transform yours too. Remember, the greatest success comes from lifting the spirits of others.

What if everything you've learned here is just the beginning? What if the real challenge lies in applying these principles in ways we've never imagined? Are you ready to embrace the unknown and lead the way?

As Peter Drucker once said, 'The best way to predict the future is to create it.' Armed with the insights and strategies from this book, go forth and create the fun, rich, and rewarding future you envision.

In this book, you've discovered the power of formulas and strategies of adding humor to marketing. The power of adding humor to your marketing in a rapidly changing world is the secret to sustainable success. Now, it's time to apply these lessons. The world of business is yours to transform.

And hey, if you're hungry for more – and who is not hungry for more humor tips and tricks for your business? – sign up for the Humor in Marketing newsletter to grow your skills with a consistent stream of examples, advertising deconstructions and inspiration. Of course your friends Zog, Byte, and Mr. Coin will be there. And maybe even a few more guides. Come by and find out.

www.AlienRobotBanker.com/newsletters or email me directly cordell@alienrobotbanker.com.

🎖 Ready, set, don't forget...